COLOR·A·

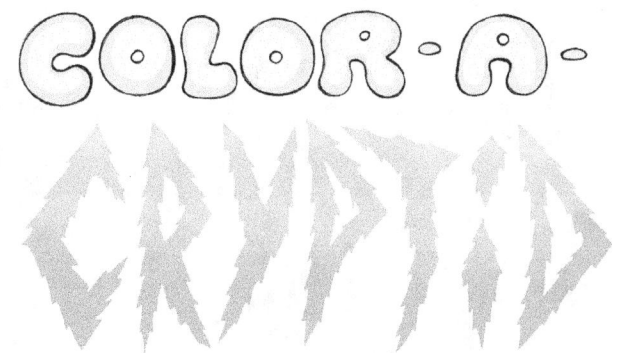

Cryptid (pronunciation/kriptid) n.
Any creature that may or may not
exist. Sightings of various cryptids
have been reported but their
reality has never been proven.

Created by:

Nathan Stapleton—McKinzie

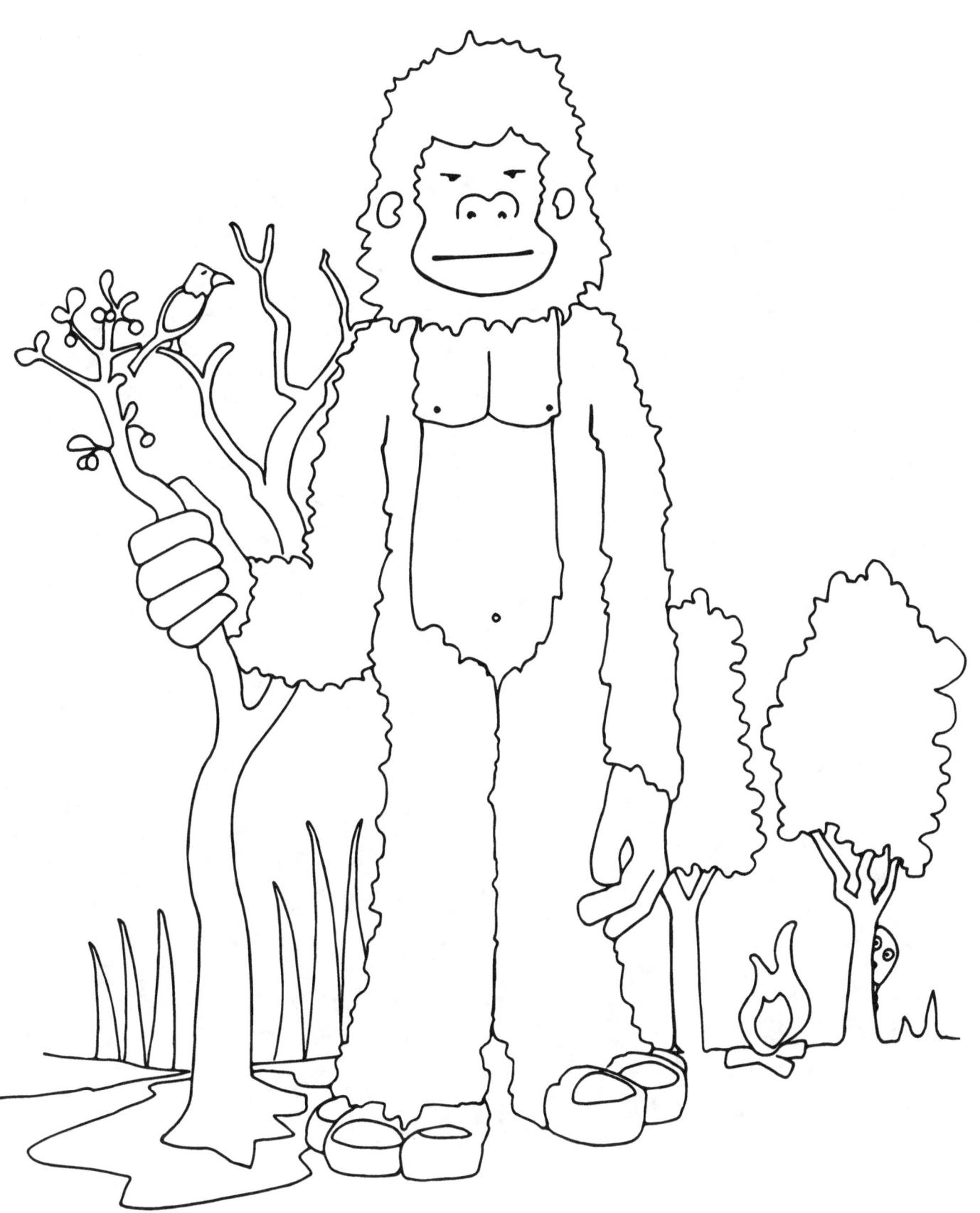

Bigfoot

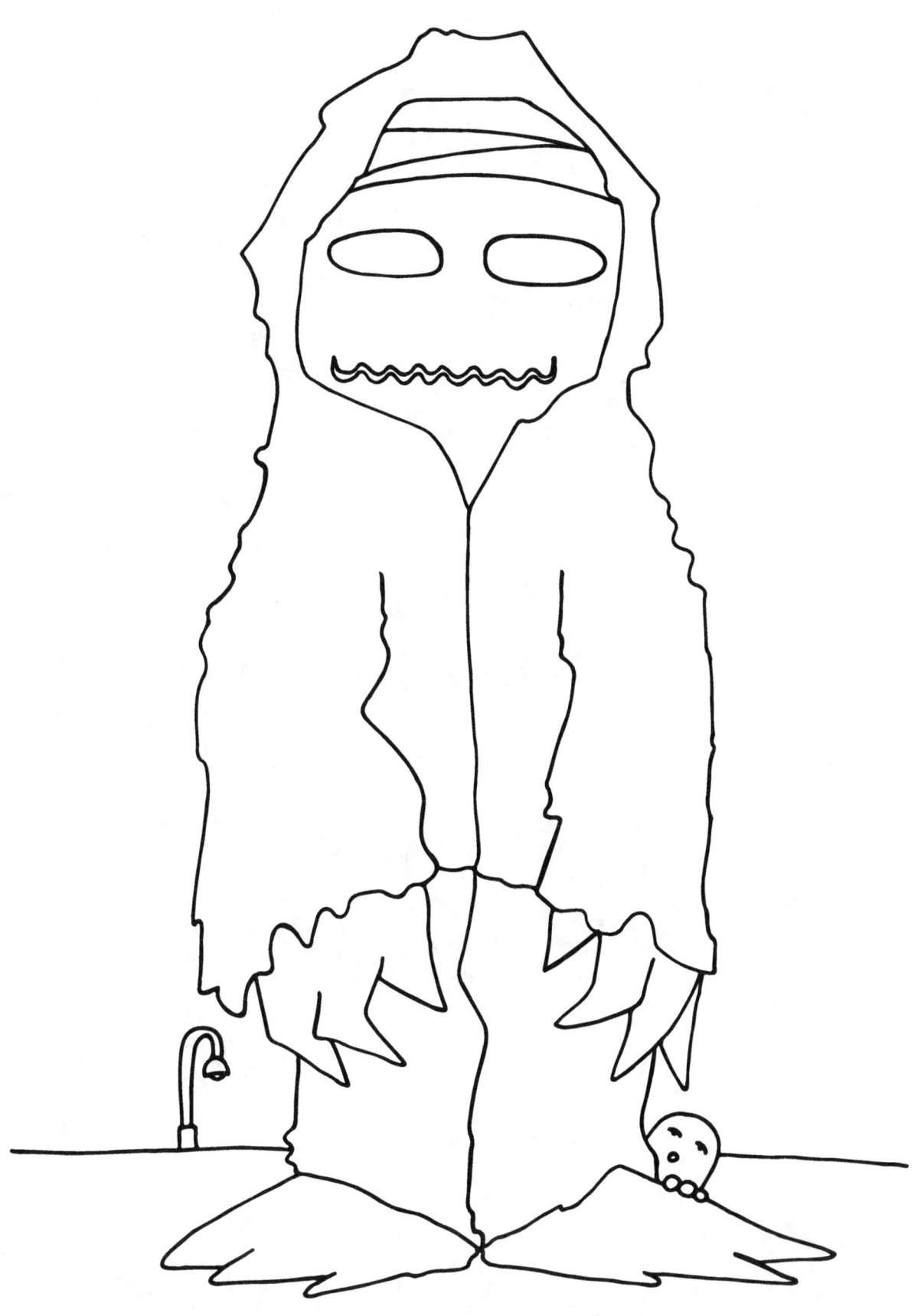

Boogeyman

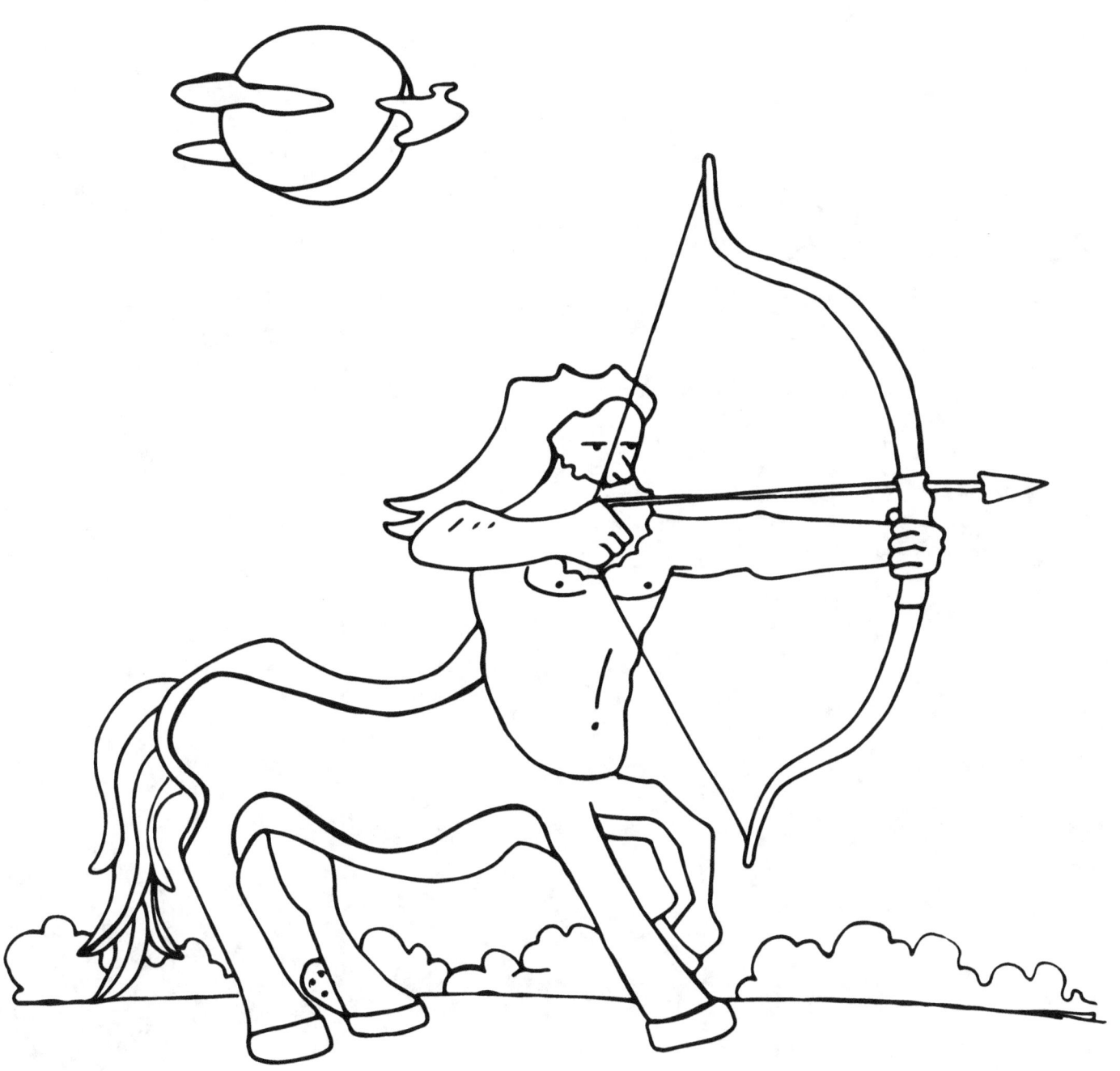

Centaur

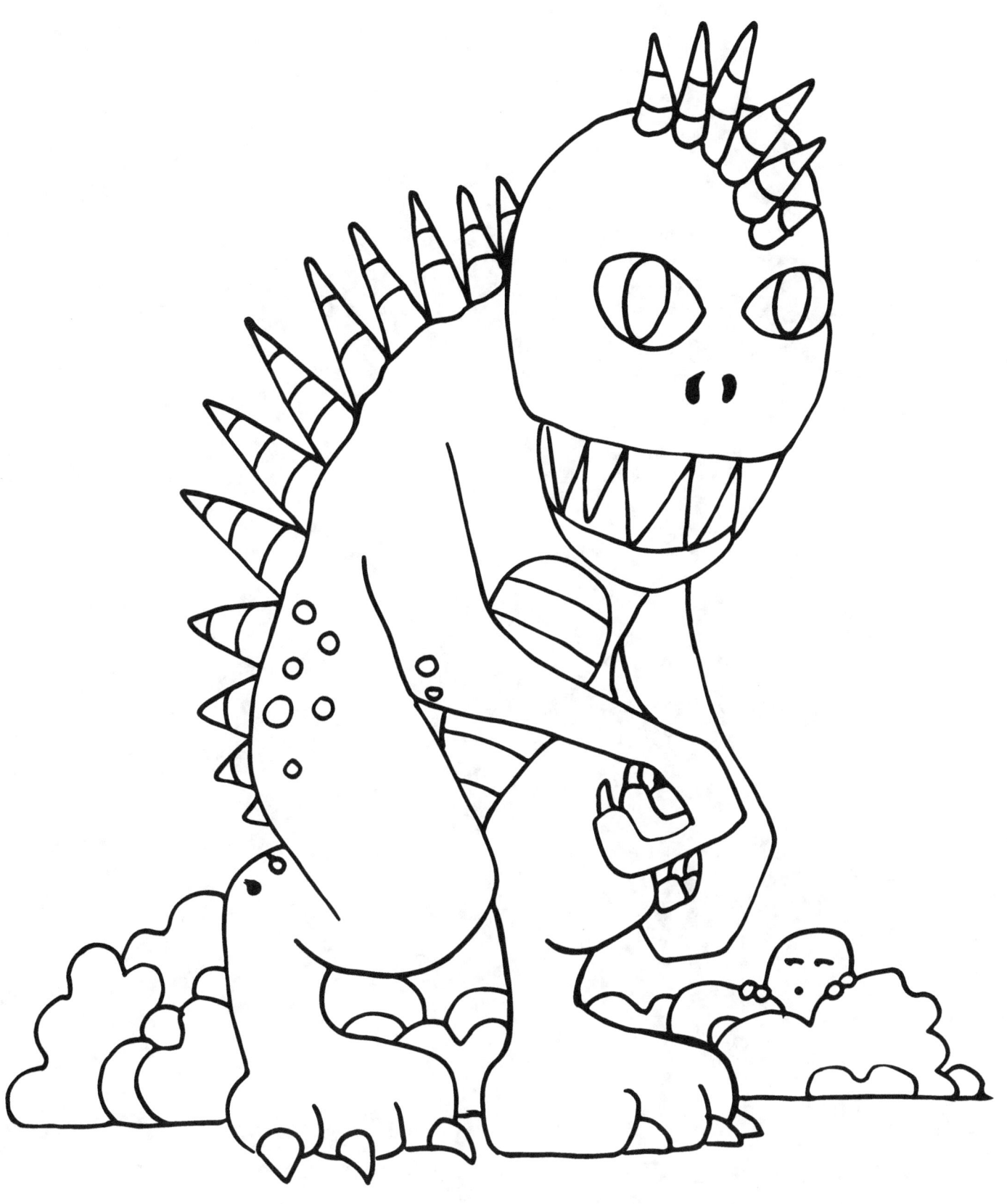

Chupacabra

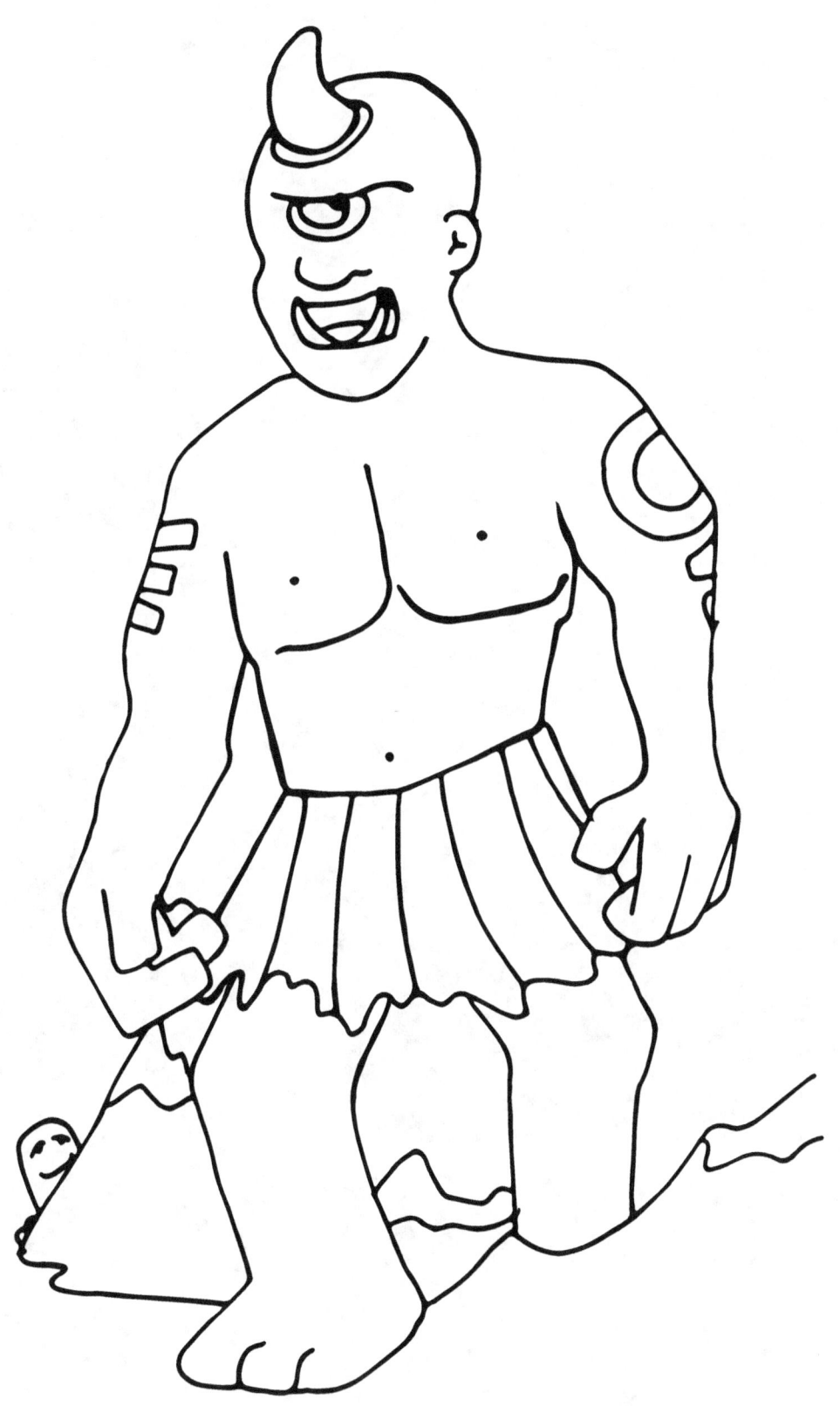

Cyclops

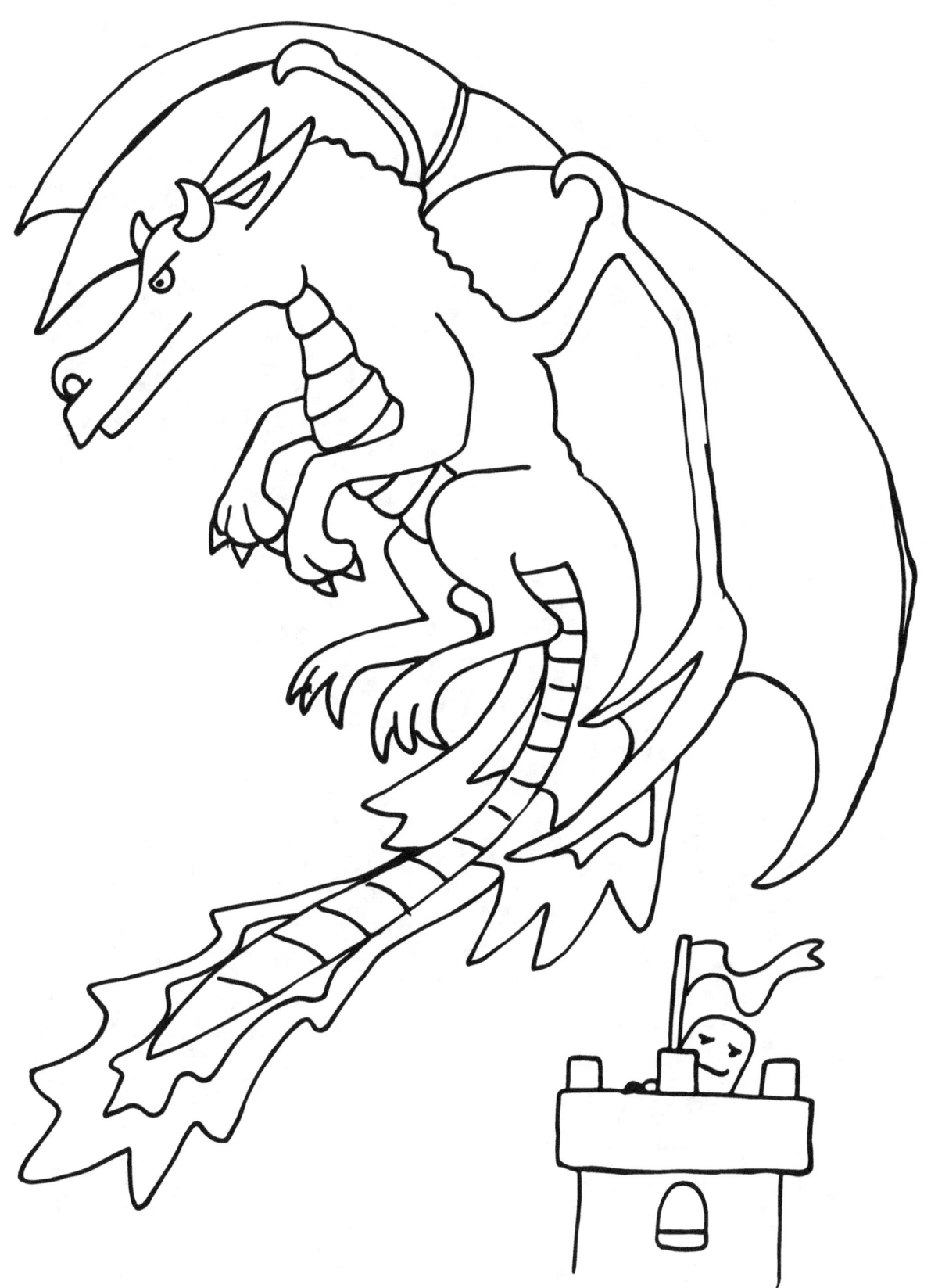

Dragon

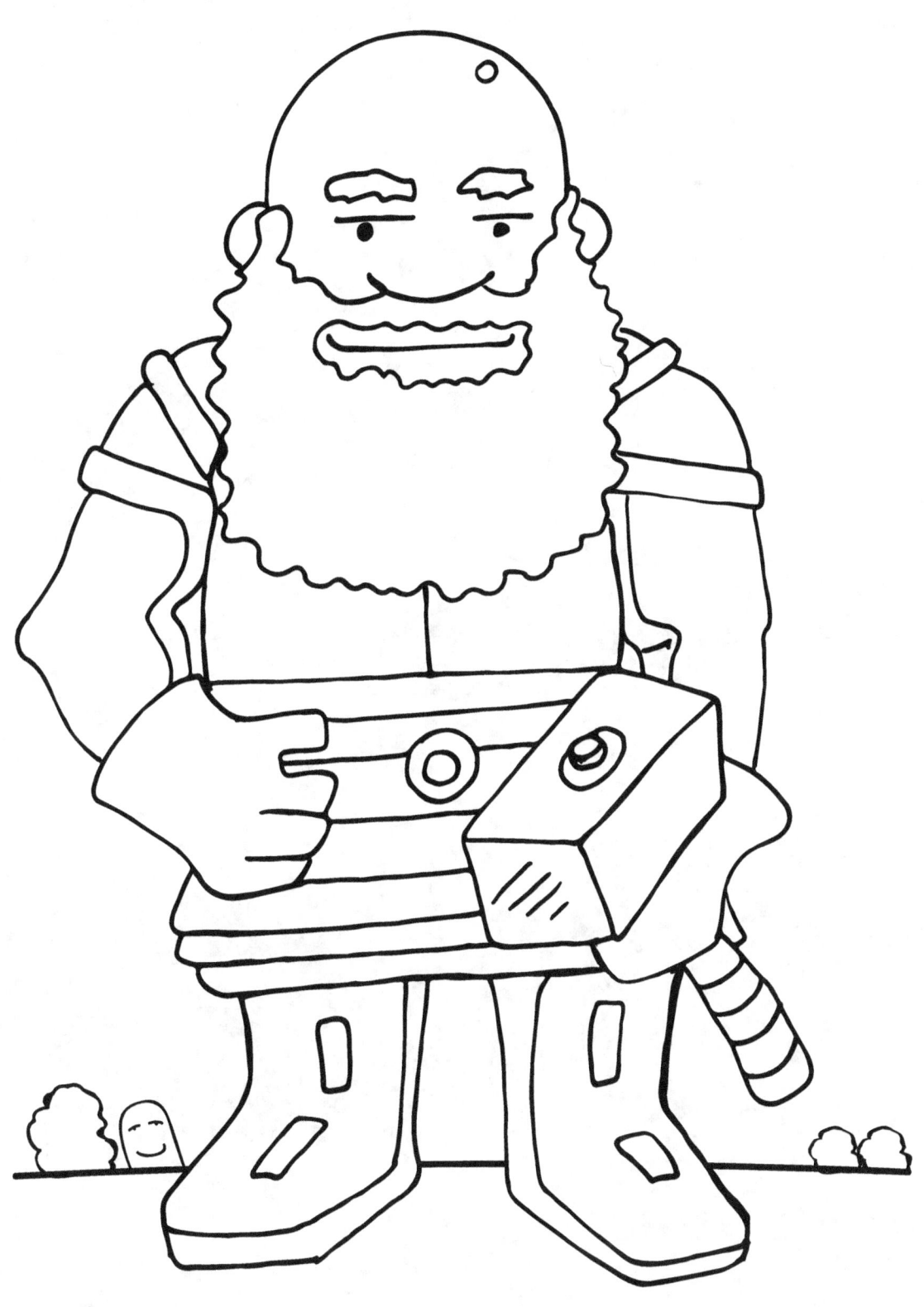

Dwarf

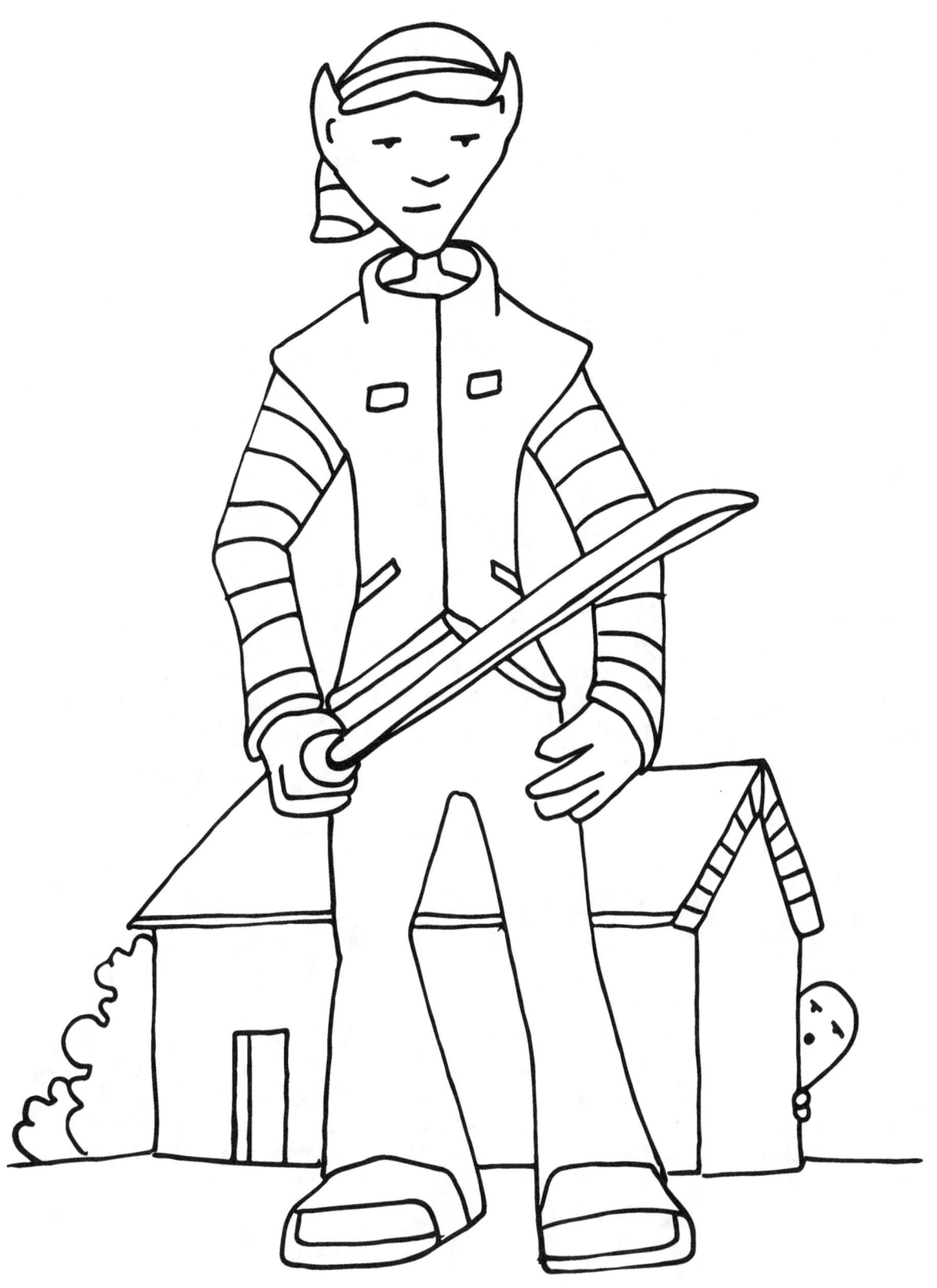

Elf

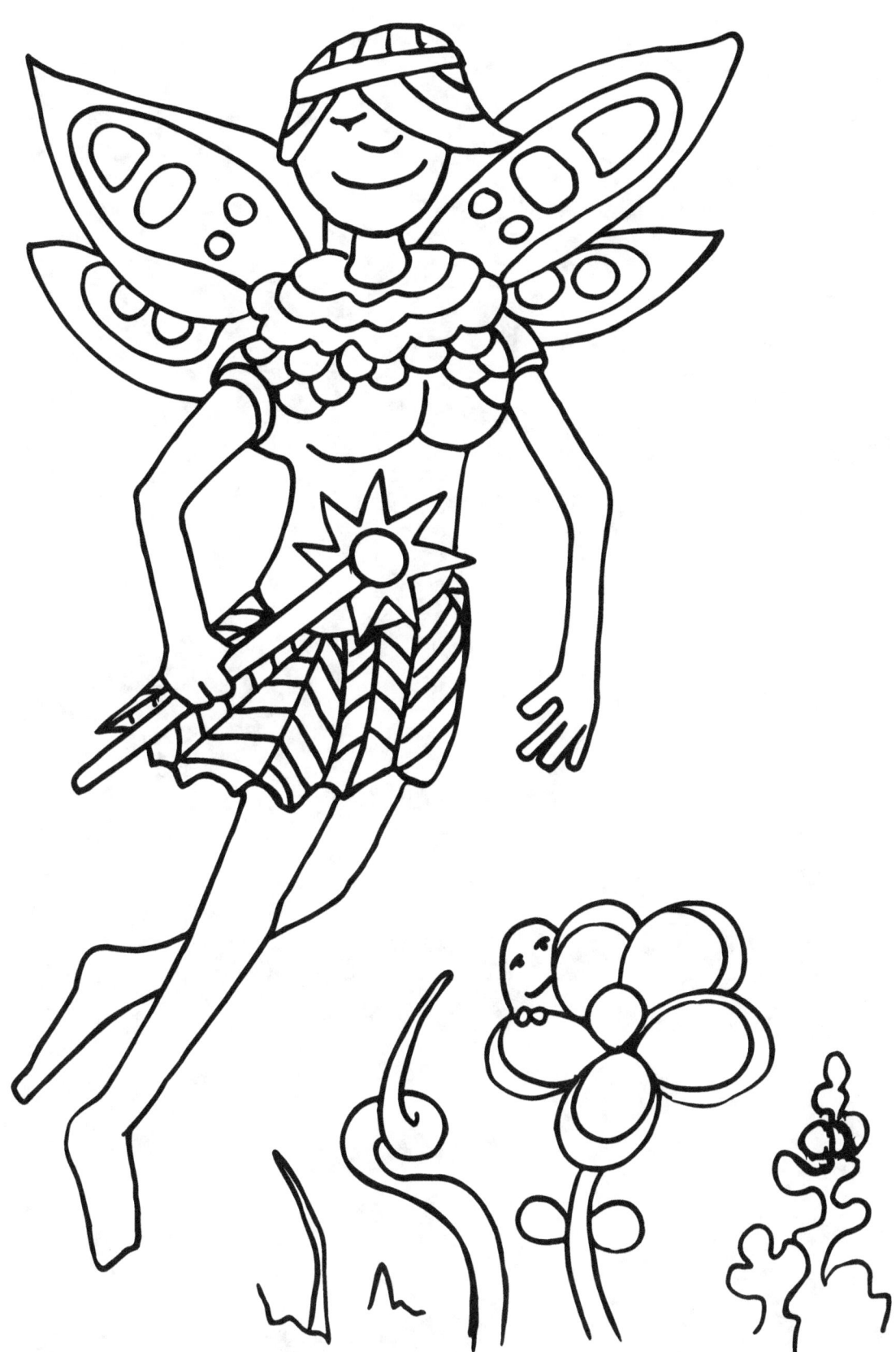

Fairy

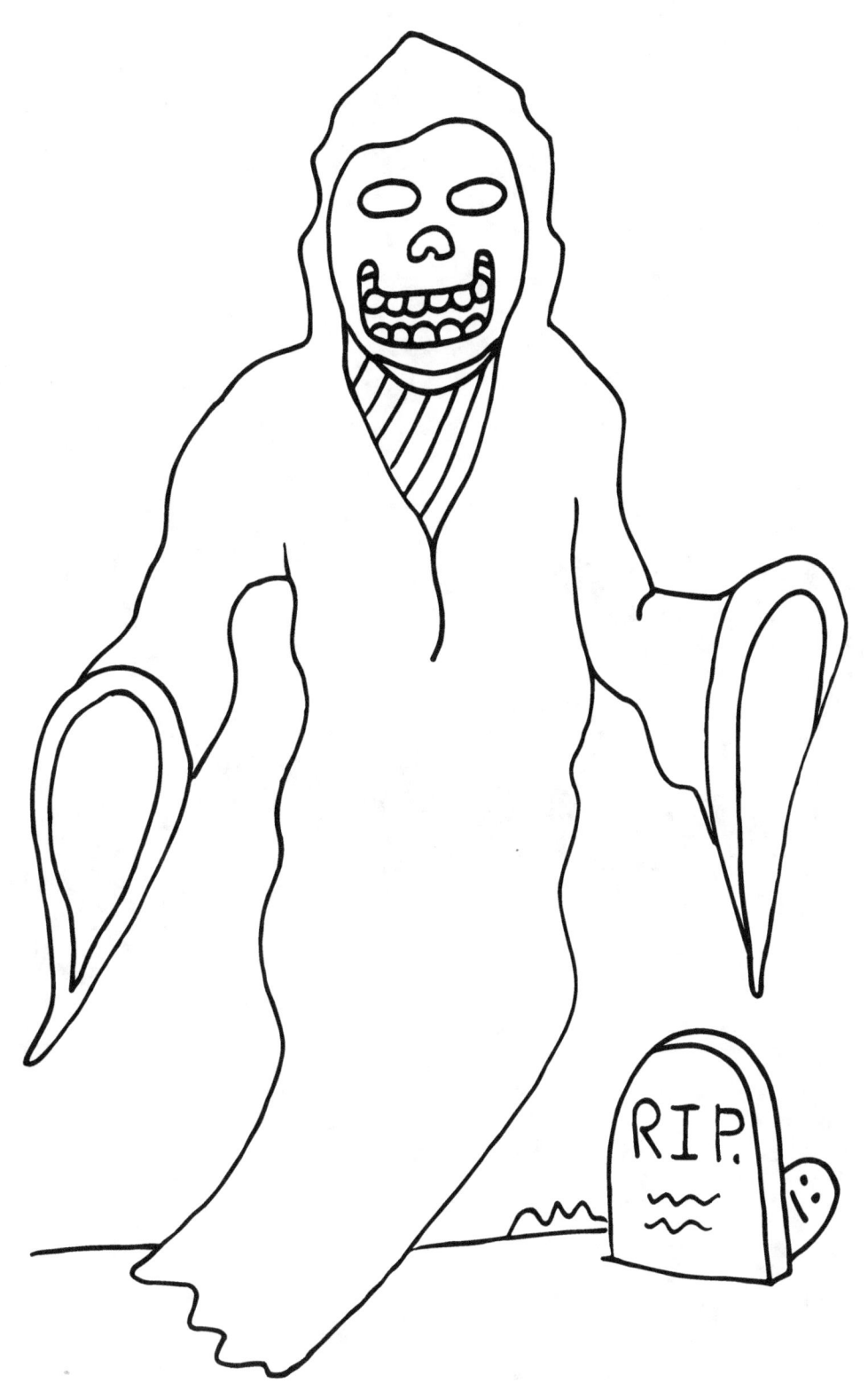

Ghost

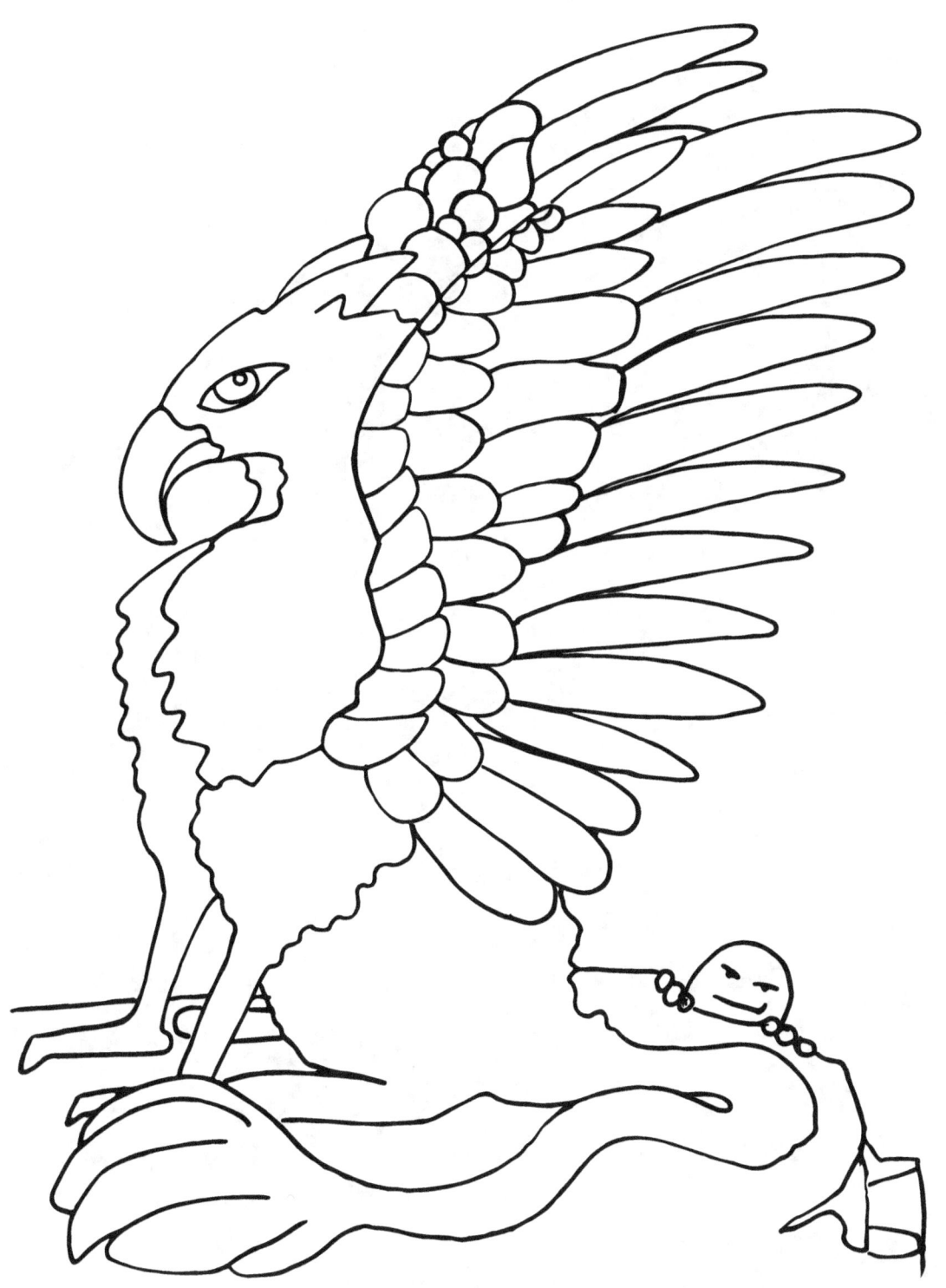

Griffin

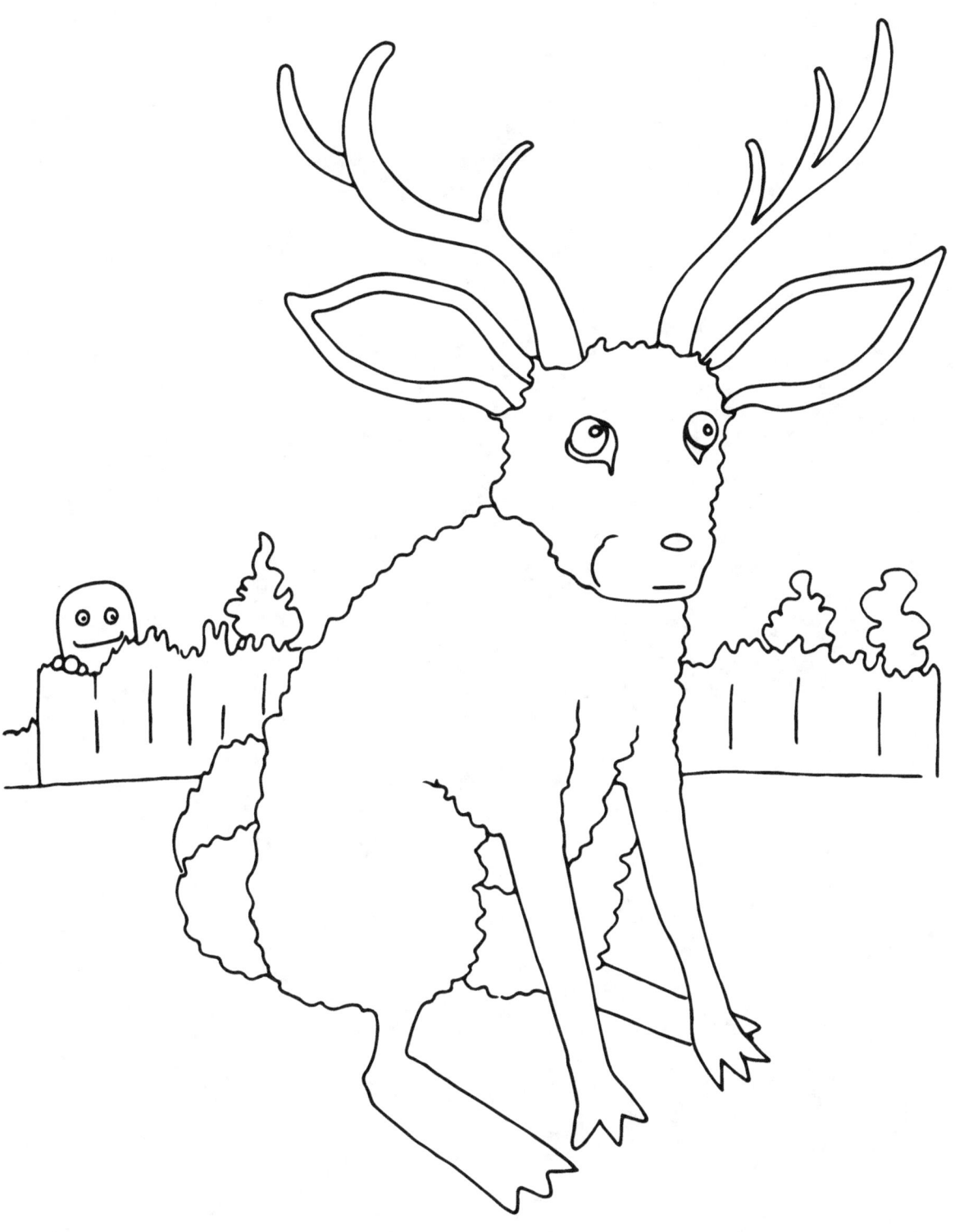

Jackalope

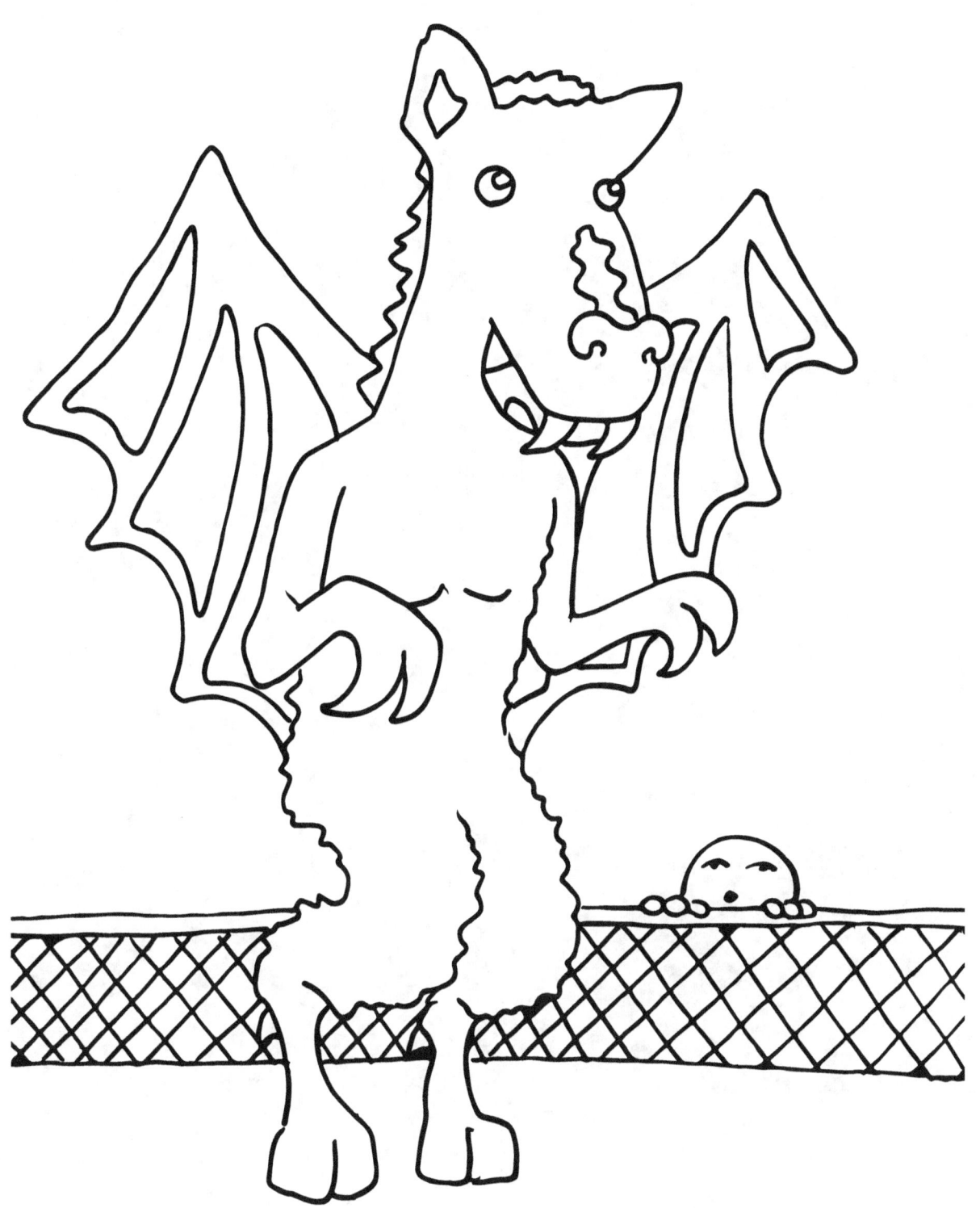

Jersey Devil

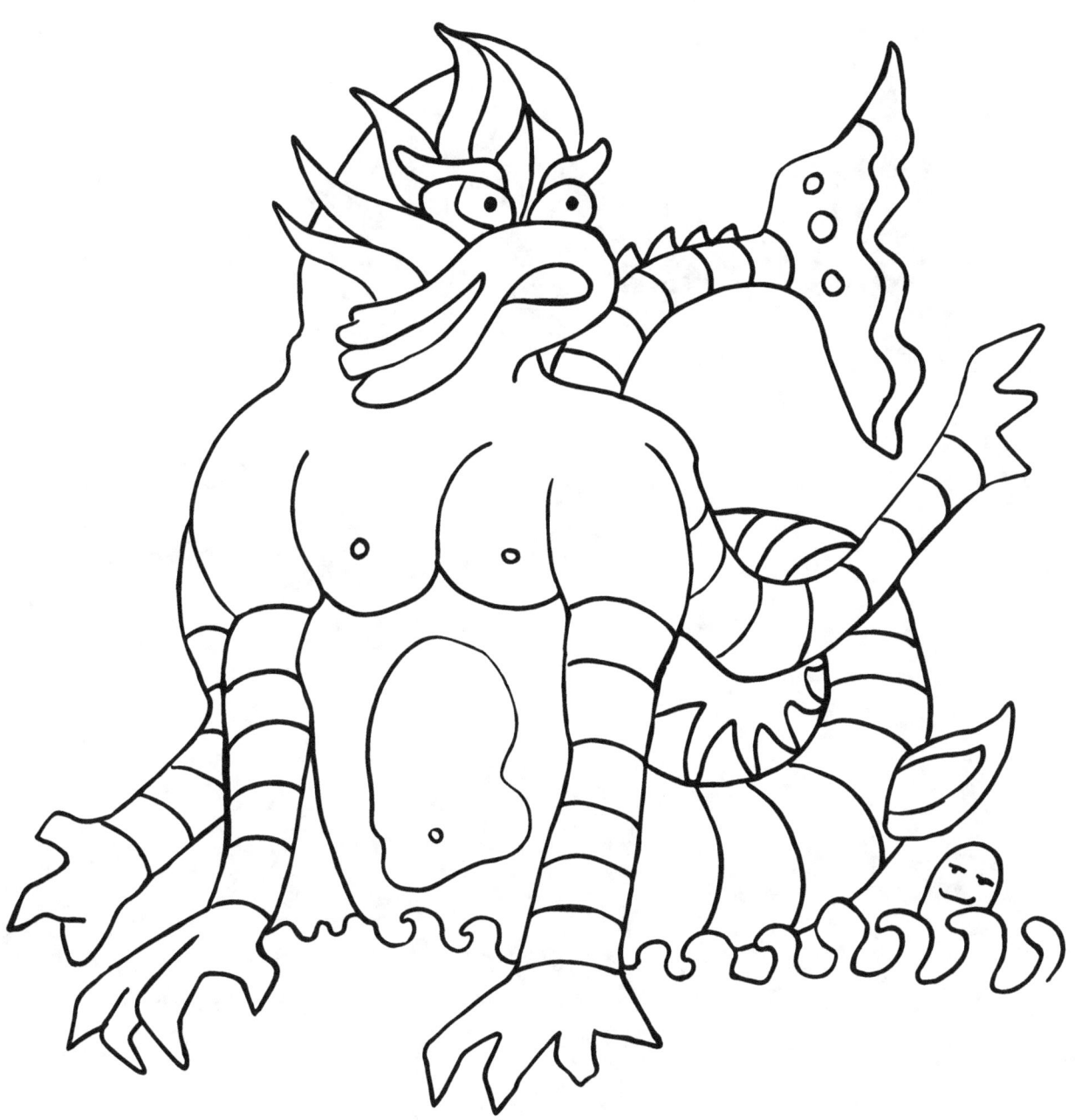

Kraken

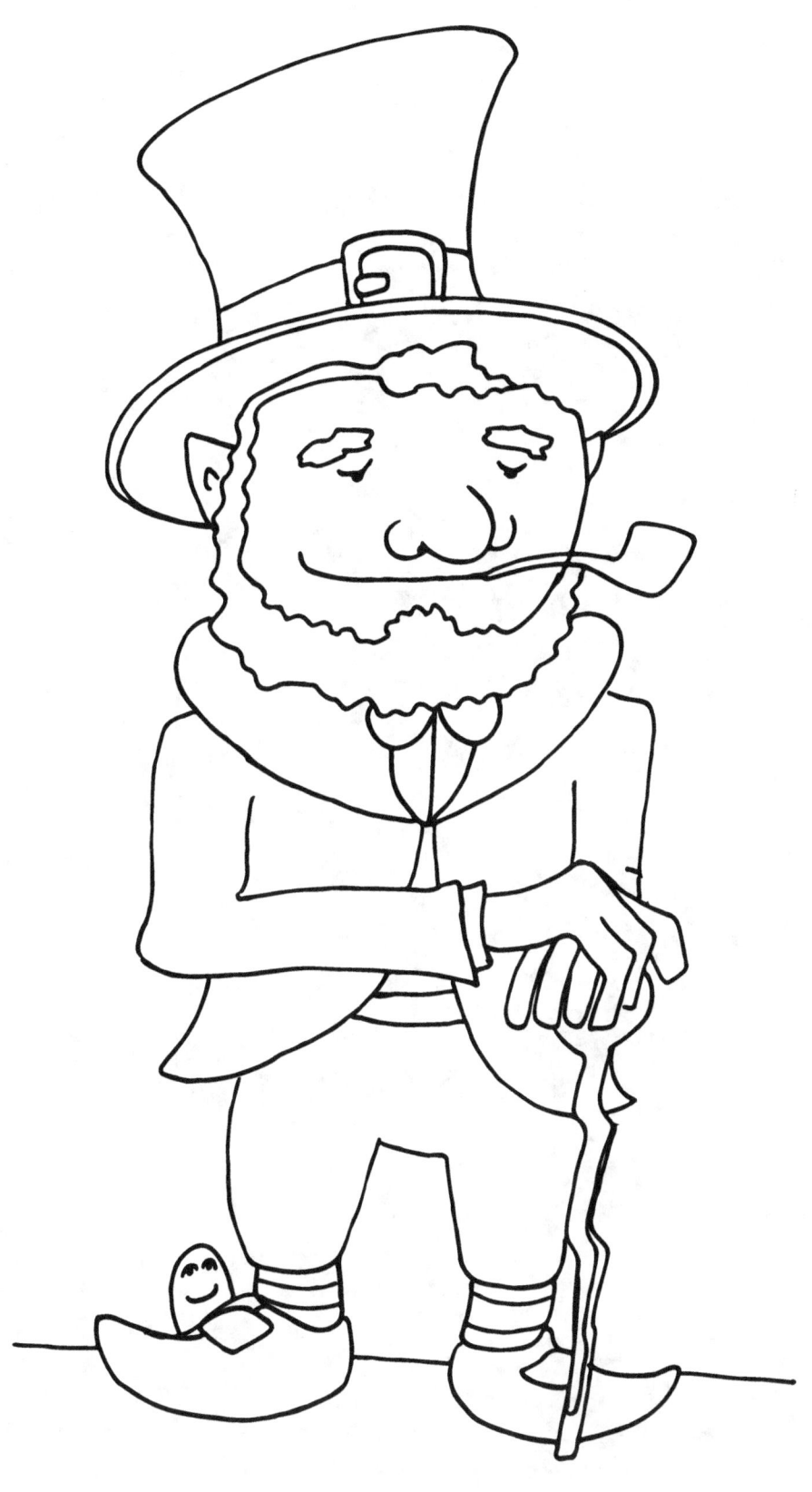

Leprechaun

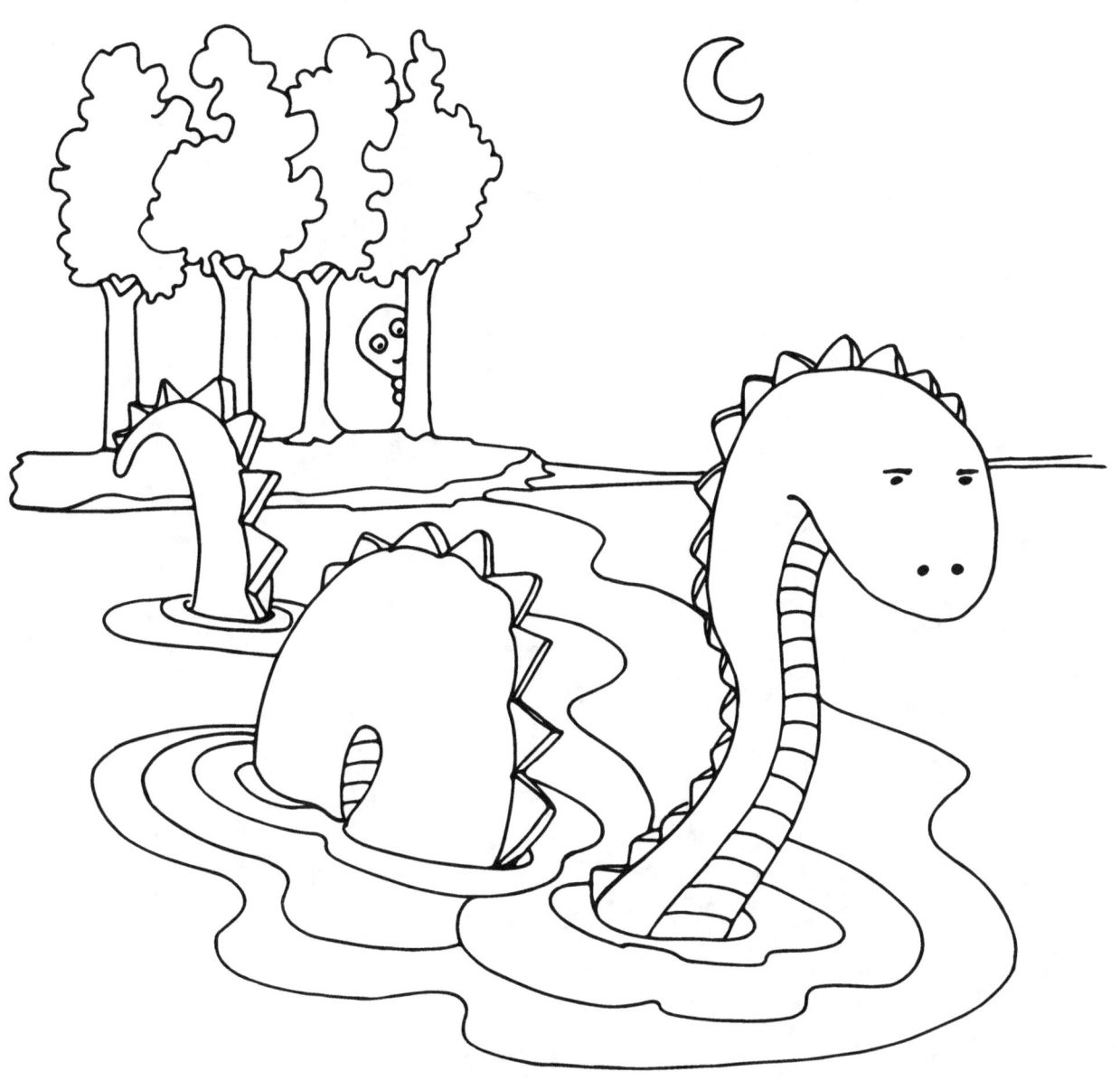

Loch Ness Monster

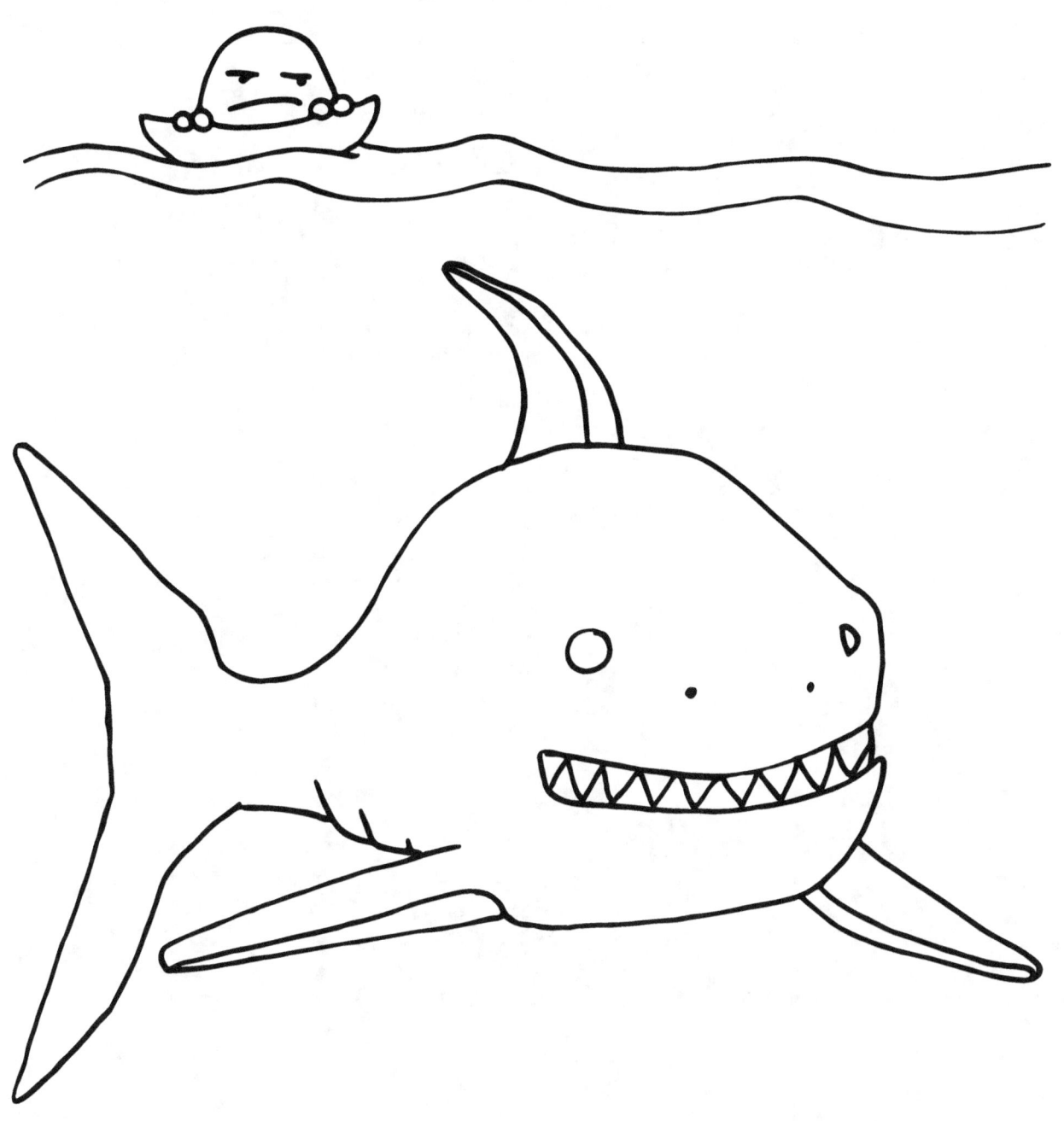

Megalodon

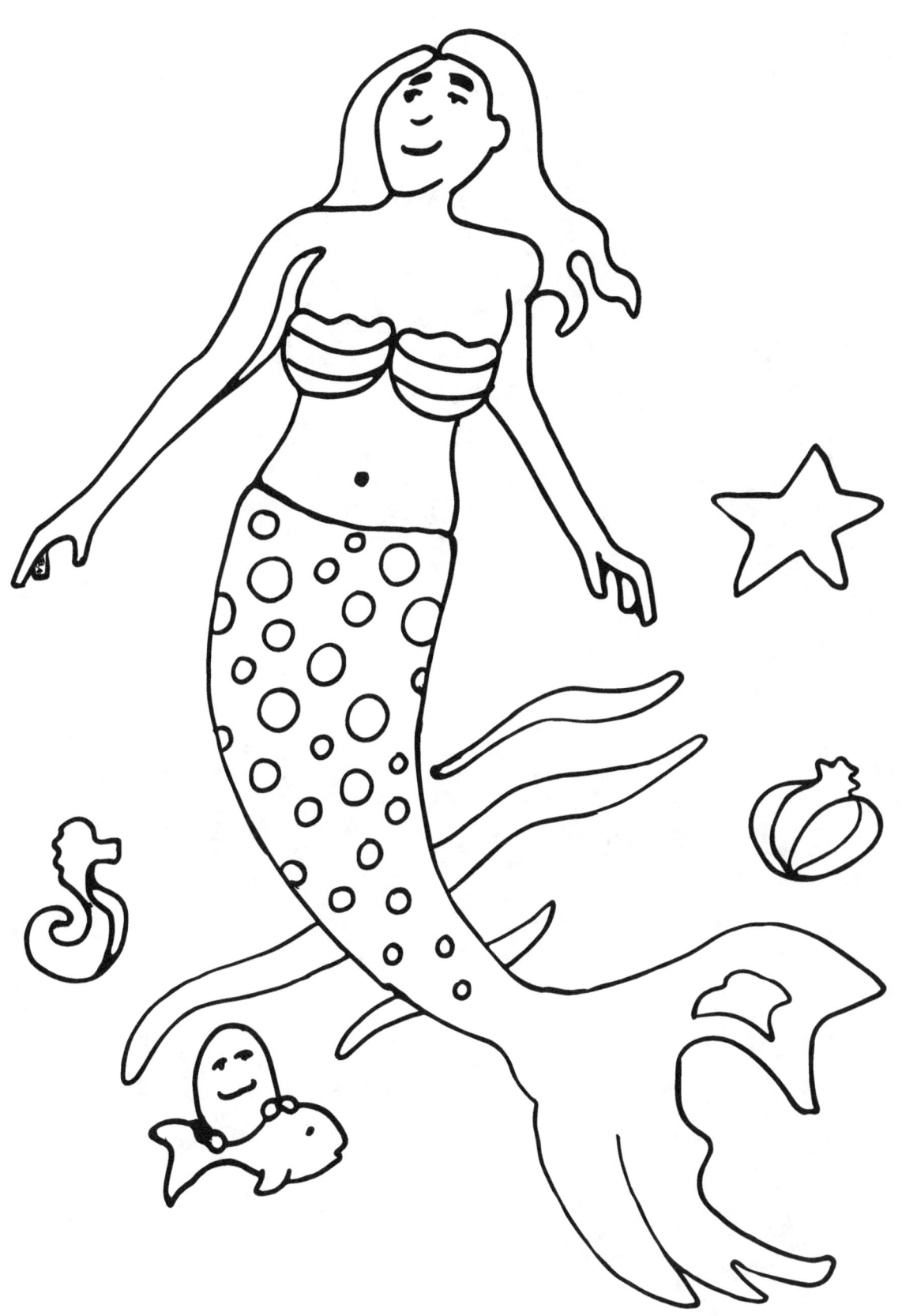

Mermaid

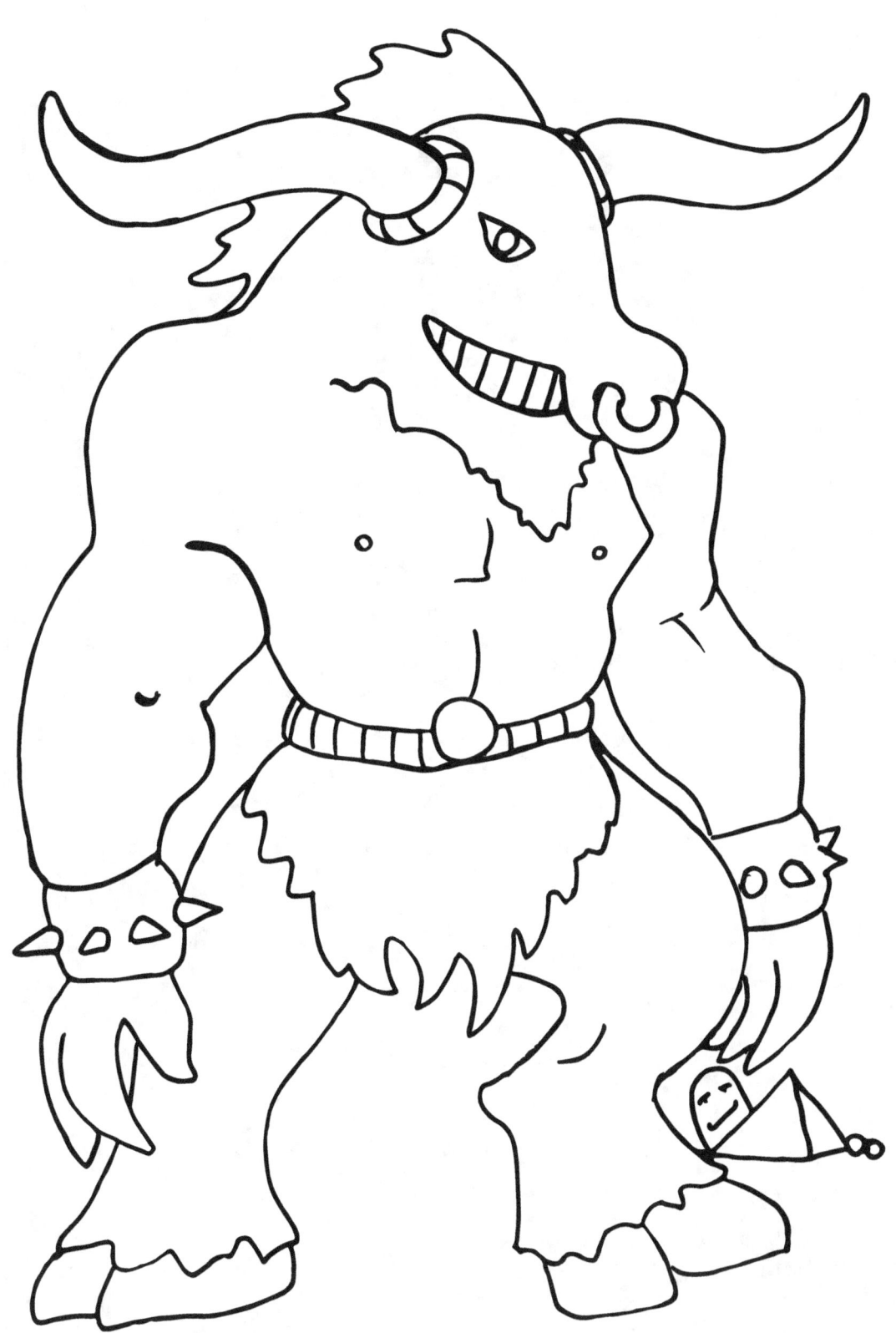

Minotaur

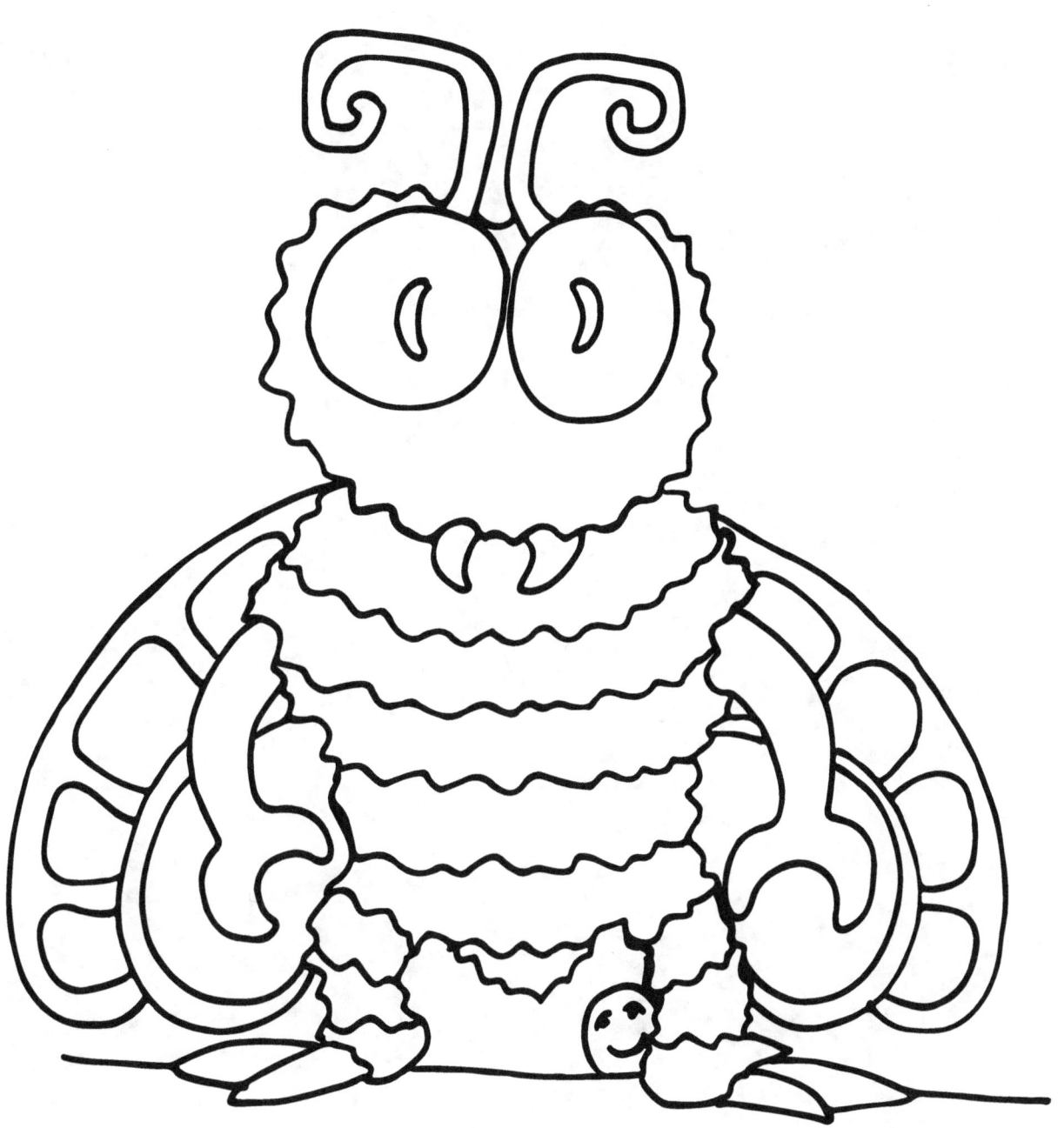

Mothman

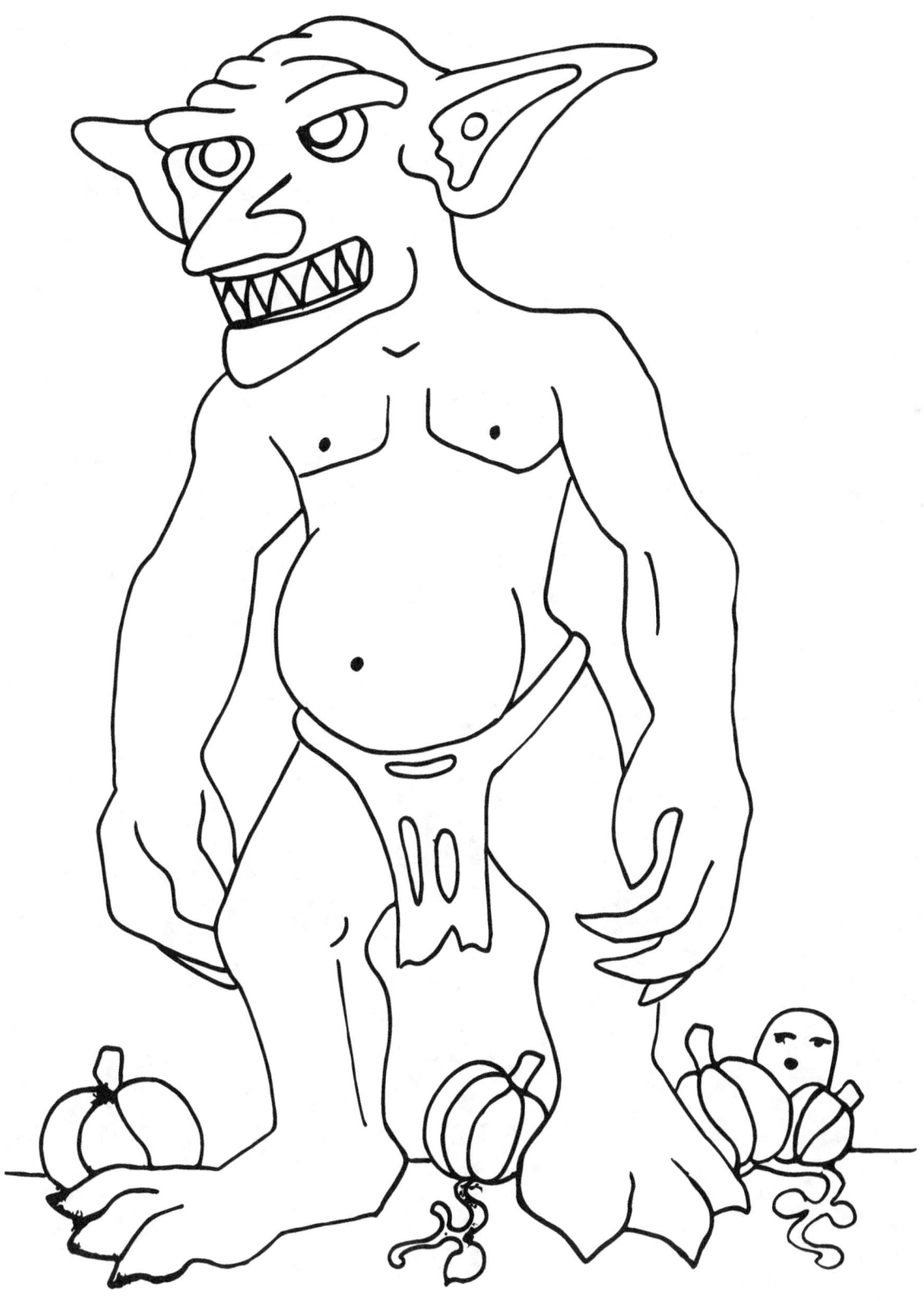

Troll

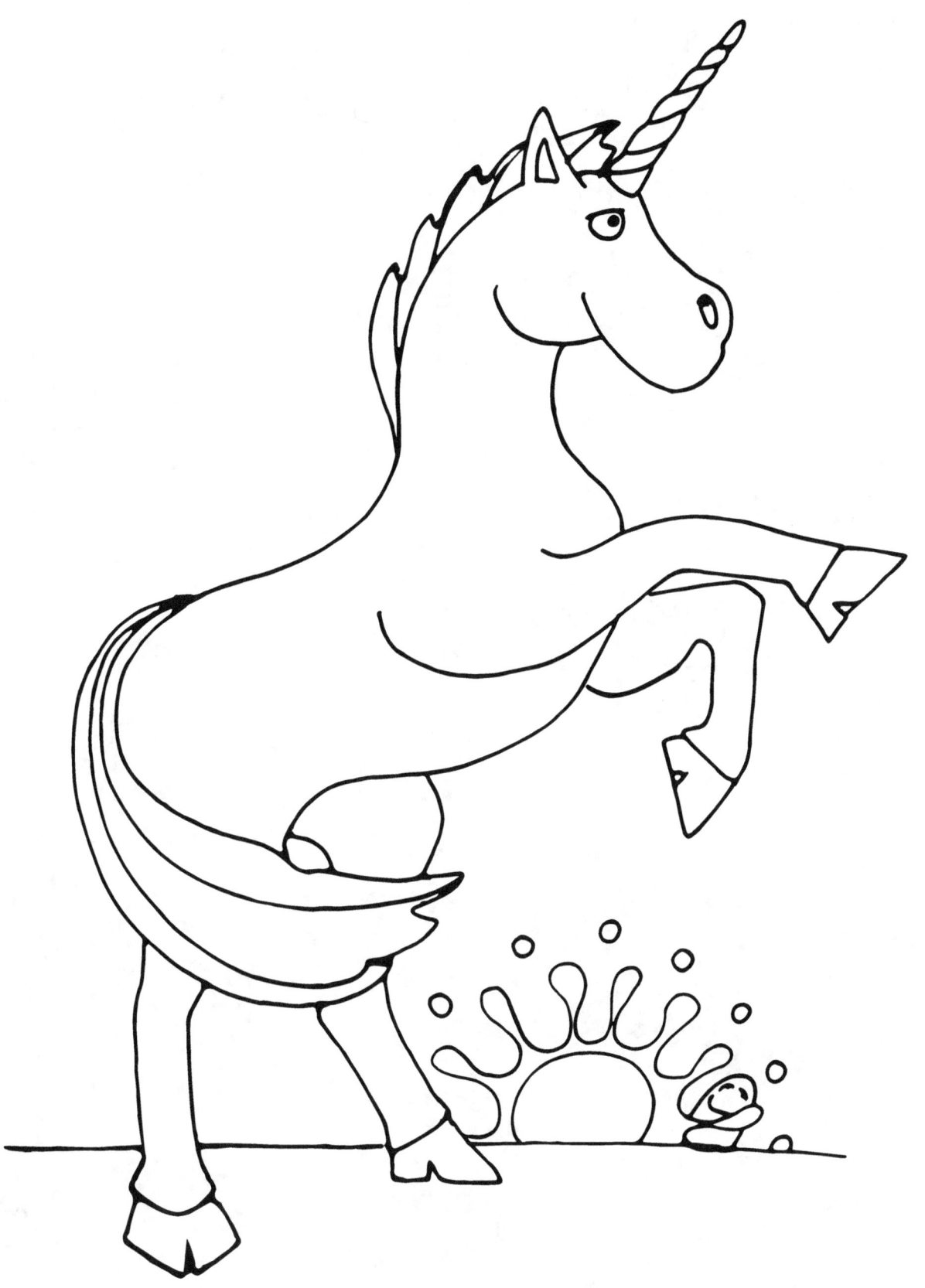

Unicorn

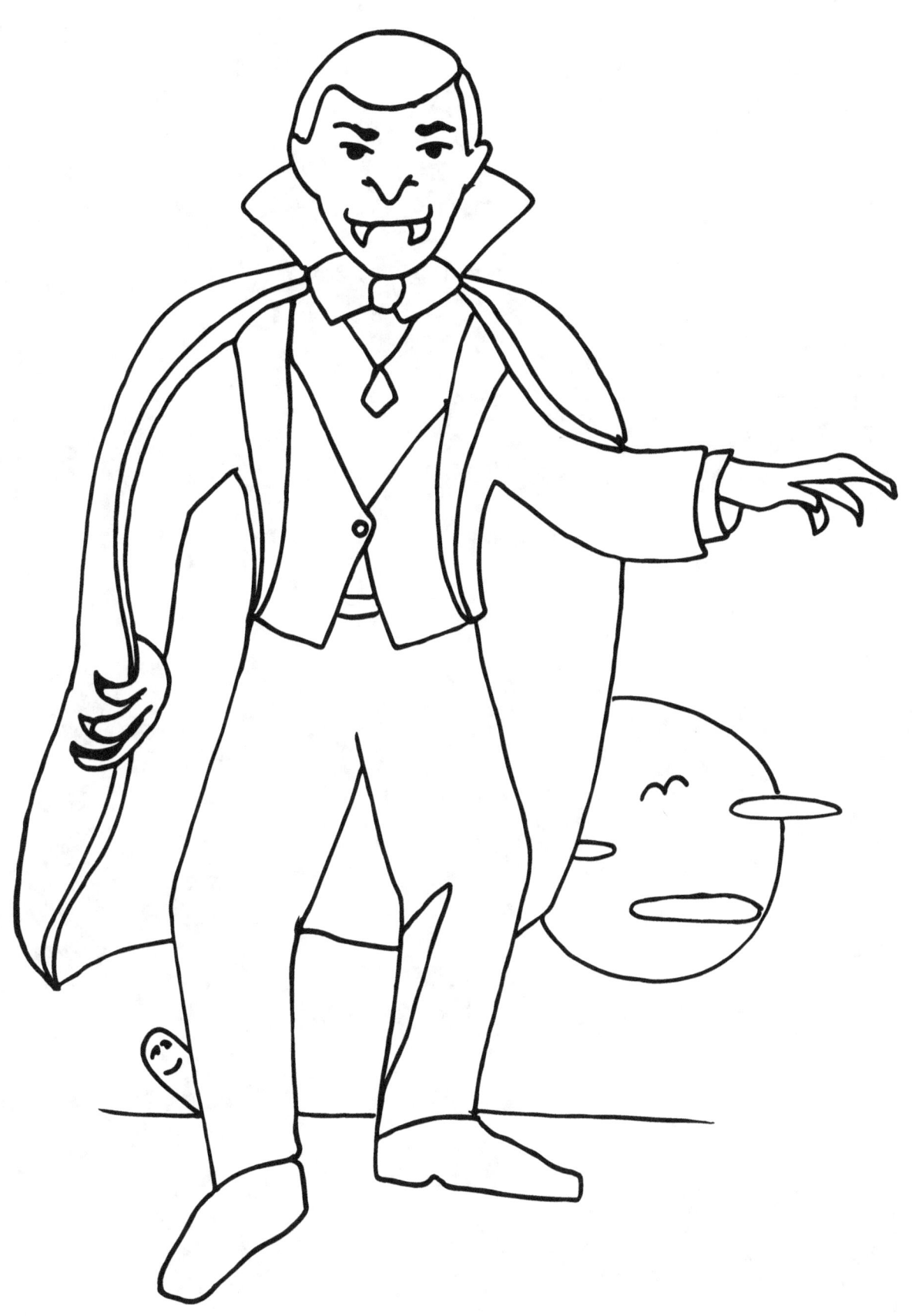

Vampire

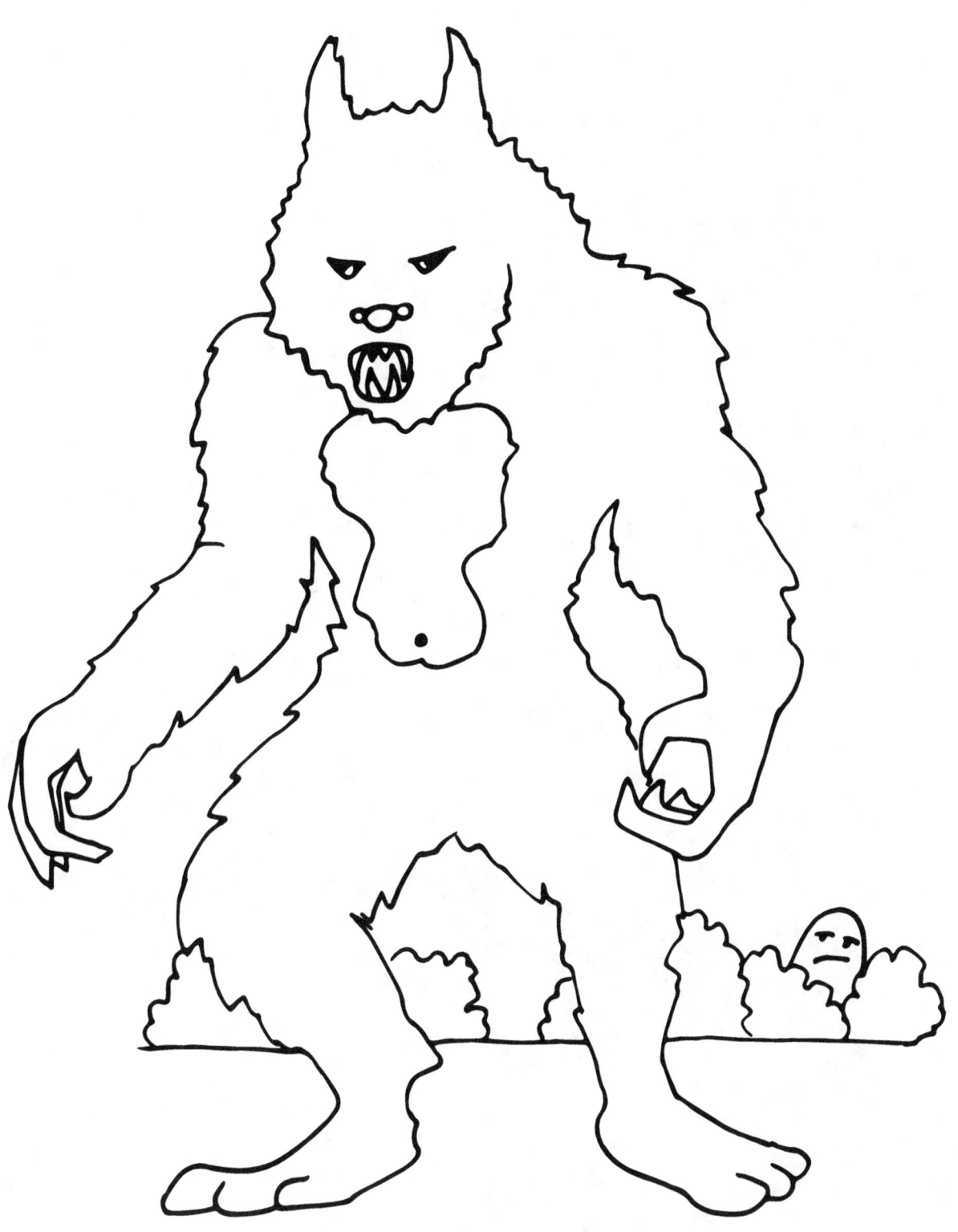

Werewolf

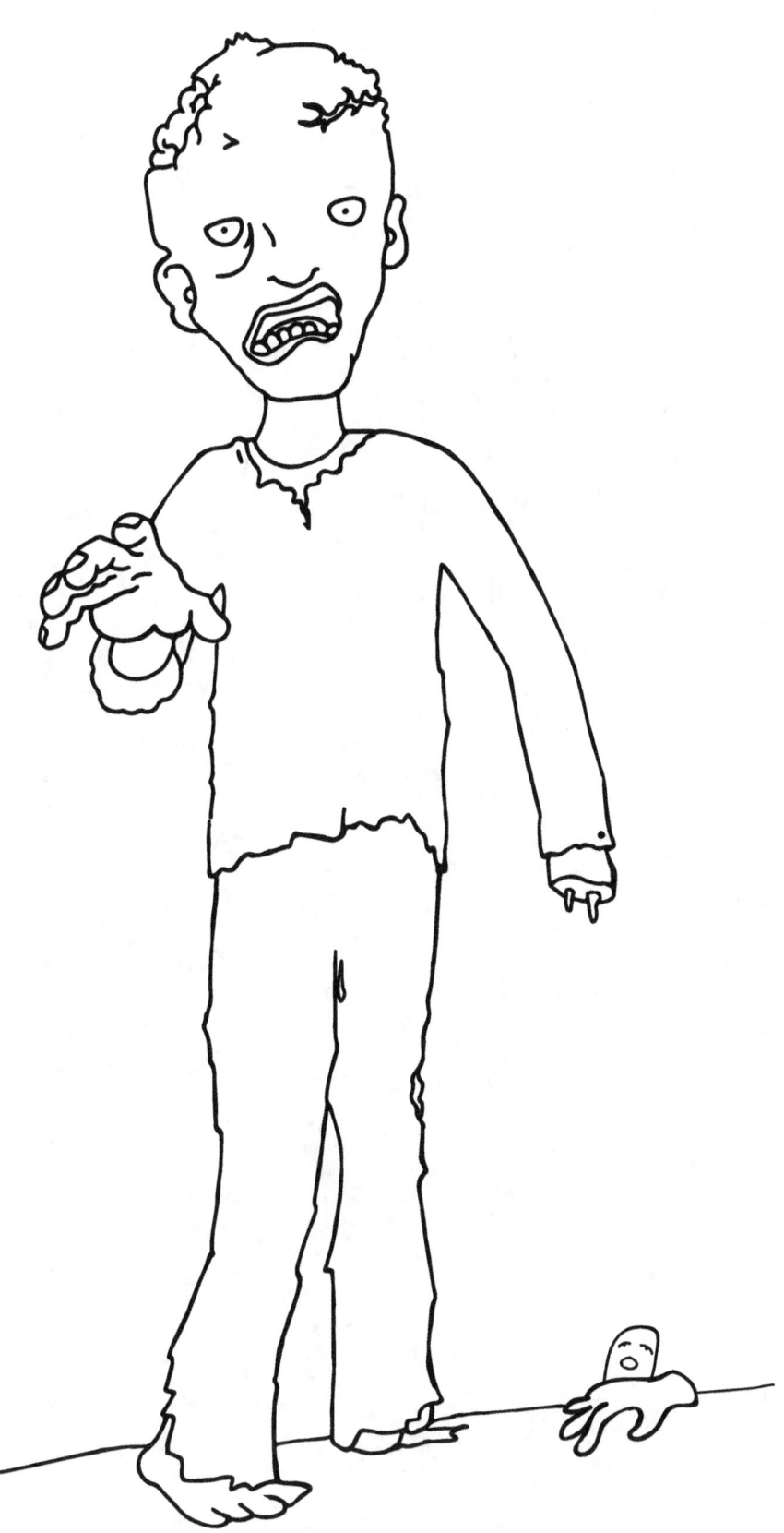

Zombie